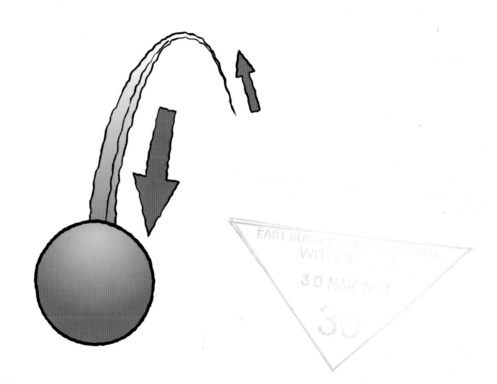

SCIENCE WORKS

DOWN TO EARTH

THE STORY OF GRAVITY

WOW!
WHAT'S
THAT ALL
ABOUT?

Jacqui Bailey Matthew Lilly

A & C BLACK · LONDON

THUD!

Zac leapt out of bed and his feet thudded to the ground. Today was THE DAY!

He hummed to himself as the hot shower water splashed down over his head.

MMM MM MMM MM...

He was too excited to eat. He grabbed his keys and jacket and headed out of the door.

HMM HMM HUM HUM...

He went on humming as he cleaned his teeth and pulled on his jeans and a t-shirt.

DA DEE DEE DA!

Hang on! Let's stop a minute and think about the things Zac has just done.

When you jump out of bed in the morning have you ever wondered what keeps your feet on the ground? Or why water always flows downwards when you turn on a shower or a tap?

FETCH, BOY!

Or why, when you throw a ball in the air, it always falls towards the ground?

The answer is a mysterious natural force called gravity.

WATCH OUT!

Gravity was first discovered in the 1660s by a scientist called Isaac Newton. He is supposed to have had the idea after he was hit on the head by a falling apple, but no one knows if it really happened that way.

Nobody really knows what gravity is, but everyone can feel it. It's there all the time, pulling you and everything else towards the centre of the Earth.

Gravity keeps your feet on the ground. It's why things roll downhill, or fall when you let them go. Without it, everything that isn't fixed to the ground would float away — and so would the air we breathe and the water in the oceans.

The drive to work didn't take long. Zac parked his car and headed for the main office. Everyone was busy and bustling about. It was always like that on Launch Day, but today was even more special for Zac. Today he was making his first flight into space.

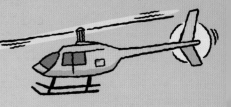

Zac had been training to be an astronaut for years. He had worked hard to keep himself fit.

He had gone through all kinds of physical tests to make sure his body could cope with the difficulties of being in space.

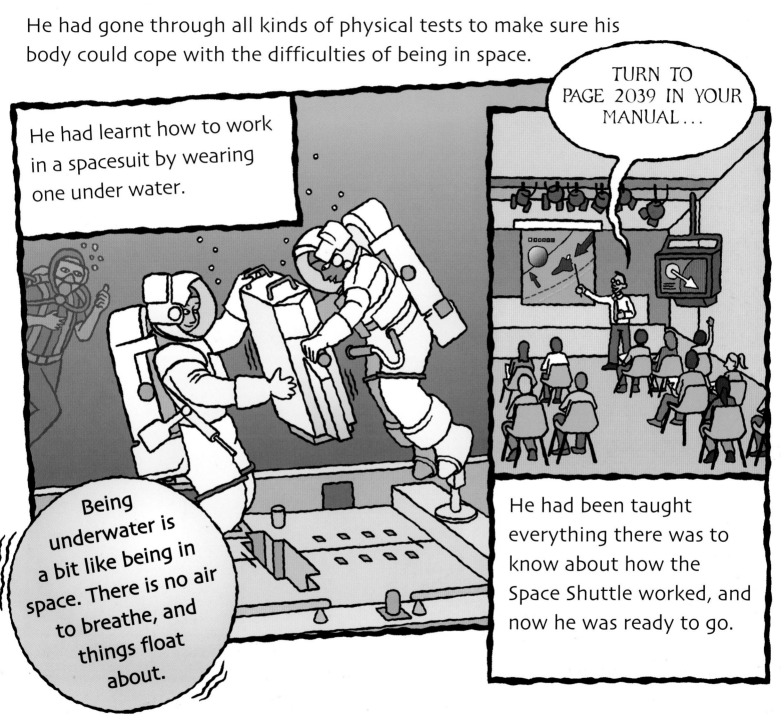

He had learnt how to work in a spacesuit by wearing one under water.

TURN TO PAGE 2039 IN YOUR MANUAL . . .

Being underwater is a bit like being in space. There is no air to breathe, and things float about.

He had been taught everything there was to know about how the Space Shuttle worked, and now he was ready to go.

Zac changed into his work clothes and met up with the rest of the crew for breakfast. They were all excited, even though some of them had been into space before.

TOMORROW, BREAKFAST IN SPACE!

Zac knew he had hours to wait before the launch — that wouldn't happen until much later.

In the meantime, the medical staff gave the crew a final check-up to make sure they were still healthy, and recorded their weight.

What we call weight is actually gravity pulling down on all the stuff that makes up your body.

When scientists talk about how much stuff something is made of — whether it's a feather, an elephant or you — they use the word mass.

WOW, YOU'RE REALLY MASSIVE!

Mass is not the same as size. Something can be small and heavy because it has a lot of mass. An apple is heavier than a balloon, for example, because it has more mass than the balloon.

At last it was time for the flight crew to board the Shuttle. One of the ground crew strapped Zac into his seat and gave him a thumbs up.

"Okay?"

Zac nodded nervously.

The crew waited while the final checks were made. Then the Shuttle's rockets roared into action and everything shook as it lifted off the launch pad.

HERE WE GO . . .

To get into space, a spacecraft has to travel fast enough and far enough to escape the pull of Earth's gravity.

WHAT WAS THAT?

This means it must reach a speed of 40,000 kilometres per hour — more than five times faster than the fastest aircraft — and climb to about 300 kilometres above the Earth's surface. To do this, the Shuttle has to ride piggy-back on a pair of very powerful booster rockets.

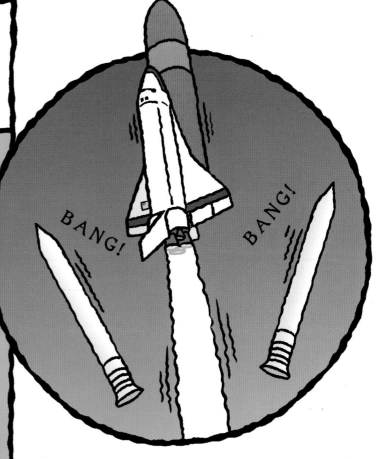

Two minutes after lift-off, the Shuttle was 45 kilometres above the Earth.

BANG! … BANG!

The two booster rockets were used up. They dropped away and fell back to Earth.

The Shuttle went faster and faster. It was speeding up so quickly it made Zac feel three times heavier than normal. He felt as if a giant hand was pressing him into his seat.

The main engine shut down and a few seconds later there was another loud bang. This time the giant fuel tank fell away.

BANG!

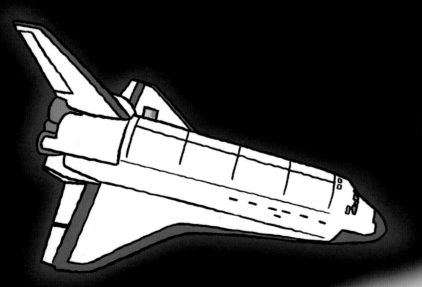

Small rockets in the tail hissed as they boosted the Shuttle even higher. Then suddenly everything went quiet. Zac was in space.

Everyone breathed a sigh of relief and released their seatbelts. Zac floated up from his seat and his head touched the ceiling.

Someone bumped into him and he felt himself bounce away towards the opposite wall.

"Sorry," said Anna.

Zac reached for a strap to hold on to. He was feeling a bit spacesick, but he knew it wouldn't last. It was just his body getting used to being weightless.

ISN'T THIS GREAT?

I THINK I'M GOING TO BE SICK.

The further you travel from Earth, the less Earth's gravity pulls on you. So although your body still has the same mass, it has almost no weight. Because you are weightless you can float around in any direction. There is no 'up' or 'down' in space.

Soon it was time to get to work. Zac's job on the flight was to find out how animals are affected by the lack of gravity.

He had rats and fish on board the Shuttle and he needed to make sure they were all right after the launch.

ARE YOU HUNGRY?

Hours later, Rory, the pilot, tapped Zac on the shoulder. Suddenly he felt starving. He grinned at Rory and followed him to the galley.

Zac chose orange juice, prawn cocktail, beef with vegetables and chocolate pudding. He added water to each container and warmed up the beef in the oven.

MMMM... ALL MY FAVOURITES!

To save storage space on the Shuttle, most of the food and drink is dried and water is added before it is eaten. The water is squirted through a tube so none of it escapes to float around the cabin.

When the food was ready Zac put the containers on a tray along with his knife, fork and spoon. Velcro strips held everything in place.

Zac strapped the tray to his knees.
He had to make himself eat very slowly.
If he grabbed at his food too fast it moved away from him!

It wasn't only the astronauts who were weightless — everything else was too. When Zac let go of his fork it stayed in mid-air until he got hold of it again.

After a few days, Zac got used to life on board the Shuttle.

He learnt how to sleep in a sleeping bag that was hung from a wall.

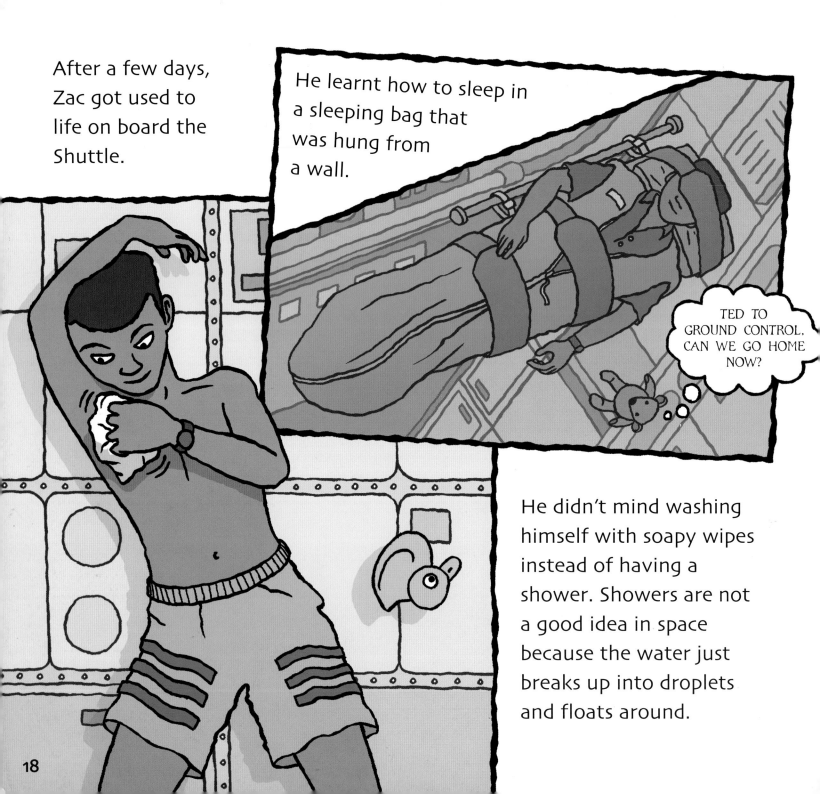

TED TO GROUND CONTROL, CAN WE GO HOME NOW?

He didn't mind washing himself with soapy wipes instead of having a shower. Showers are not a good idea in space because the water just breaks up into droplets and floats around.

He got quite good at fixing himself onto the toilet with his feet on the footrests and two bars pulled across his legs. Even weeing into a cup-shaped funnel wasn't too bad!

IT'S NICE TO GET A FEW MOMENTS' PEACE.

It is vital to stop waste or dirt floating about in a spacecraft. On the Shuttle any solid or liquid waste goes straight into special containers or bags, where it is stored and taken back to Earth.

WOW!

The one thing he never got used to was seeing the Earth from space. He loved to watch the bright colours of his planet as it rolled beneath him.

Zac also liked looking at the Moon. From the Shuttle he could clearly see the shadows and shapes on its shiny face.

The Moon travels on an endless journey around and around our planet. Earth's gravity holds it in place like a ball on the end of an invisible piece of string.

TIDE'S COMING IN!

Moon

Earth

But the Moon has gravity too, and although its gravity is weaker it is still strong enough to affect the Earth. It is the Moon's gravity pulling on our oceans that makes the tides rise and fall.

Two weeks raced by and Zac was amazed when it was time for the Shuttle to return to Earth. Suddenly everyone was busy cleaning up the crew areas and packing away their equipment.

Zac strapped himself to his seat and took a last look at space. It was littered with millions of stars like grains of sugar on a black tablecloth.

The Shuttle dived back into the atmosphere. This is the layer of air that surrounds the Earth.

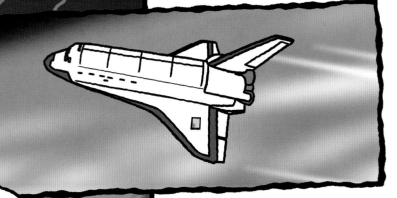

WOW! THIS IS GETTING HOT!

When something moves through air it rubs against the stuff that air is made of. This rubbing action is called friction. The Shuttle was falling so fast that friction made its surface glow red hot. It also slowed the Shuttle down.

Rory guided the Shuttle towards the landing site and everyone held their breath.

As the wheels touched the runway, a parachute billowed out behind it. Air filled the parachute and pushed it backwards.

CAAAW!

The open parachute pulled against the Shuttle, helping to slow it down before it reached the end of the runway.

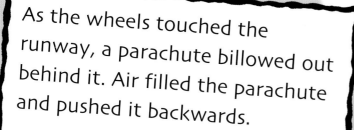

Everyone cheered. They were glad to be safely home, but Zac knew that all of them would leap at the chance to go into space again.

RESISTING GRAVITY

Things fall because gravity pulls them downwards, but not everything falls in the same way. A leaf floats gently to the ground, while an apple hits it with a thud. The pull of gravity is the same on both of them, but the leaf falls more slowly because of its shape.

A leaf has a flat thin shape. When it falls it traps more air underneath it than the apple. The air pushes up against the leaf and slows it down. The air is resisting, or pushing against, the pull of gravity. If the apple was thin and flat like the leaf it would fall slowly too.

STANDING UP

We use our bones and muscles to resist the pull of gravity. Without them we would not be able to lift ourselves off the ground. In space, an astronaut's body does not have to work against gravity. In fact, over time, astronauts can become as much as 5 centimetres taller in space because the bones in their spine spread out.

Astronauts exercise every day while they are in space. Otherwise their muscles would be too weak to hold them up when they got back to Earth.

Floating About

Living without the pull of gravity takes some getting used to. Astronauts cannot eat bread or biscuits in space in case the crumbs float into a piece of machinery. Instead they make their sandwiches from tortillas — a kind of chewy pancake.

Astronauts with long hair keep it tied firmly back. Otherwise it can float out around their head like seaweed in the ocean.

THIS IS MORE FUN THAN A TRAMPOLINE!

Moonwalking

All really massive objects have a force of gravity that can be felt. The Sun and the other planets have gravity. Even the Moon has it, but because the Moon is smaller than the Earth its gravity is much weaker. When astronauts are on the Moon, they weigh six times less than they do on Earth — and they can jump six times higher.

TRY IT AND SEE

FLOATING ON AIR

How something falls on Earth depends on its shape. A crumpled ball of paper will fall faster than the same piece of paper when it's flat. This is because of the resistance of air. Parachutes use air resistance to slow an object's fall, or to slow its speed along the ground.

Try making your own toy parachutes to see how it works.

You will need:
- A plastic bag
- Cotton thread
- Some sticky tape
- A pair of scissors
- A ruler
- Some small plastic toys

1 Cut two squares out of the plastic bag. Make one piece about 20 cm square, and the other one about 30 cm square.

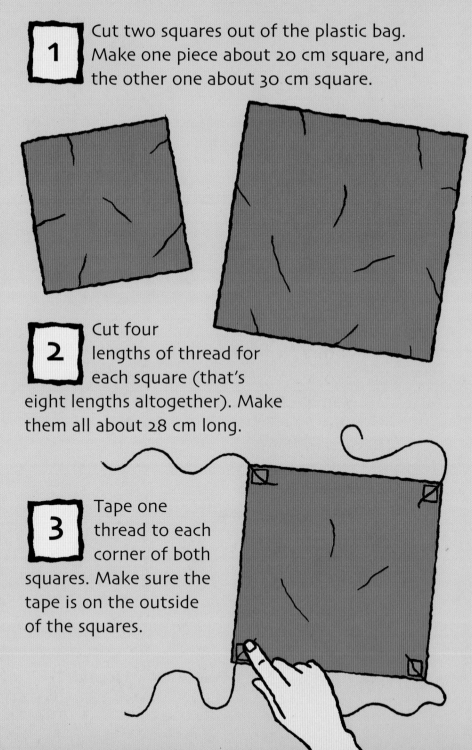

2 Cut four lengths of thread for each square (that's eight lengths altogether). Make them all about 28 cm long.

3 Tape one thread to each corner of both squares. Make sure the tape is on the outside of the squares.

4 Collect up the ends of each set of four threads and loop them into a knot to keep them together.

5 Choose three plastic toys of roughly the same size and weight. Take two of the toys and tie or tape each one to the knotted end of a parachute.

6 Take the two parachutes and the third toy to a safe high spot, such as the side of a staircase. Or stand on a sturdy chair. MAKE SURE AN ADULT IS WITH YOU. (If you are outside it's best to do this when there is no wind, otherwise your parachutes could get blown away.)

Drop the toy on its own first of all. Count how long it takes to hit the ground. Now drop each of the parachutes in turn. How long does each parachute take to land? Is there a difference between them?

The fastest to fall is the toy on its own. The slowest should be the larger parachute.

Try cutting a small hole in the top of one of the parachutes. Does this make a difference to how it falls?

WHO SAID PIGS CAN'T FLY!

FORCEFUL FACTS

In space, any dust inside the Shuttle just hangs in the air. It gets into the astronauts' eyes and makes them sneeze.

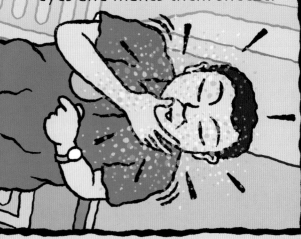

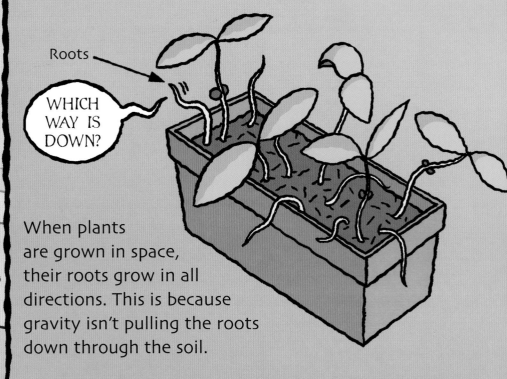

Roots

WHICH WAY IS DOWN?

When plants are grown in space, their roots grow in all directions. This is because gravity isn't pulling the roots down through the soil.

You are 15 grams heavier at the North and South Poles than at the equator. This is because the Poles are slightly nearer to the centre of the Earth. If you could stand at the centre of the Earth you would be weightless.

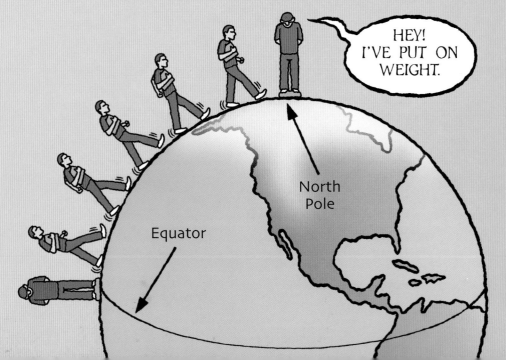

HEY! I'VE PUT ON WEIGHT.

North Pole

Equator

INDEX

SOME SPACEY WEBSITES TO VISIT

http://kids.esa.int = the European Space Agency's website for kids has puzzles, quizzes, info and lots of good stuff about space, the universe and everything. http://spaceplace.jpl.nasa.gov/en/kids/ = one of NASA's websites for kids, with games, projects and fun stuff. Or go to www.nasa.gov/audience/forkids/home/index.html for links to more sites. www.exploratorium.edu/observatory/index.html = find out your age and weight on other worlds, along with lots of other cool stuff.

For Chris
JB
For Finola, Holly and Bill
ML

First published in 2006 by
A & C Black Publishers Limited
38 Soho Square London W1D 3HB
www.acblack.com

Created for A & C Black Publishers Limited by
two's COMPANY
Copyright © Two's Company 2006

The rights of Jacqui Bailey and Matthew Lilly
to be identified as the author and the illustrator of this
work have been asserted by them in accordance with
the Copyrights, Designs and Patents Act 1988.

ISBN-10: 0-7136-7353-2 (hbk)
ISBN-13: 978-0-713-67353-1 (hbk)
ISBN-10: 0-7136-7354-0 (pbk)
ISBN-13: 978-0-713-67354-8 (pbk)

Printed and bound in China by Leo Paper Products

A & C Black uses paper produced with elemental chlorine-free
pulp, harvested from managed sustainable forests.